ON THE WRITING OF THE INSANE

New York

Published by Curious Publications
101 W. 23rd St. #318
New York, NY 10011
curiouspublications.com

All imagery appears as it did in the original publication of *On the Writing of the Insane*, 1870.

Report of the Medical Superintendent for the Year 1880 is reproduced from *The twenty-third annual report of the Committee of Visitors of the Cambridgeshire, Isle of Ely and Borough of Cambridge Pauper Lunatic Asylum for the year ending the thirty-first day of December, 1880.* This file is available at the Wellcome Collection.

ISBN-13: 978-1-7353201-6-8

Printed and bound in the United States of America.

A NOTE ON THE TEXT

This book was originally published in 1870. At the time, George Mackenzie Bacon was a medical superintendent at Cambridgeshire County Asylum (now Fulbourn Hospital) near Cambridge, England. The slim volume offers Bacon's observations on the idiosyncrasies of his patients' handwriting.

Bacon is also the author of *On primary cancer of the brain: an inquiry into its pathology, with statistics as to its frequency, and illustrative cases* (1865), written while serving as an assistant physician at the asylum. Brain cancer first drew his attention, as he stated in the book's preface, after unexpectedly discovering a malignant tumor "while examining the brain of a lunatic."

In September 1870, the *London Practitioner* shared a report from Bacon in which he discussed treating an "epileptic lad in whom I had reason to think the fits were mainly due to sexual excitement" by removing his testicles.

"He has considerably improved in intelligence, and is able to make himself useful in simple work," Bacon noted. "He has ceased to masturbate, and seems to have no sexual inclination, but there is no apparent effeminacy of character."

Following *On the Writing of the Insane* is Bacon's annual Report of the Medical Supervisor from 1880, featuring tales of trepanation, hydrocephaly, and more.

FRONTISPIECE

ON THE

WRITING OF THE INSANE,

WITH ILLUSTRATIONS.

BY

G. MACKENZIE BACON, M.D.,

Medical Superintendent of the Cambridgeshire County Asylum.

"An experience of wasted energies and baffled thoughts."

Lothair.

LONDON:
JOHN CHURCHILL AND SONS,
NEW BURLINGTON STREET.
1870.

PREFACE

The following pages are intended merely to furnish illustrations of the writing of the insane, and not to support any particular views.

The subject of insanity is one that is practically excluded from the observation of the public, or of the bulk of the medical profession, and it is so of necessity. For this reason I think that any simple recital of facts connected with this speciality must have a certain value, even if not leading to any direct practical issue. It has been my endeavour to place before the reader a series of pictures of insane minds, painted by themselves, and it is for him to draw what lessons he may from the study of them. Looking back myself, with the aid of some years' familiar experience of the insane, on the histories of the patients who wrote the letters I have given, it seems to me that I can recognise each case in these documents, and I hope, therefore, that others may derive some useful impressions from their perusal. The cases are meant to speak for themselves, and I have avoided encumbering them with many comments. There is no particular novelty in them, though I am not aware that any such series has been before published, and there is only one point on which I lay claim to any originality, viz.—the diagnostic value of the handwriting in general paralysis. I cannot find that anyone else has before called attention to the alteration the handwriting undergoes in this disease, and it strikes me as so distinctive as to demand consideration in the observation of such cases. I first noticed this subject in a few remarks in the *Lancet* of July 4th, 1869, in which paper the figures in Plate IV appeared. In the first place I had the writing photographed on glass, and exhibited it with an ordinary magic lantern in a dark room to the medical students of the University. By this plan the irregularities in the writing, being magnified, show more clearly still. I have no wish to attribute undue importance to this matter; but it seems to me of some value in the early stages of a disease so difficult to recognise at that period. With these explanations I leave the matter to the judgment of others.

County Asylum,
Fulbourn, near Cambridge.

ON THE WRITING OF THE INSANE

Of the three modes of communicating their ideas that human beings possess, viz., speech, gesture, and writing, the last one has received the least notice. Indeed, the study of hand-writing is more connected in one's mind with fortune-telling, and other forms of popular superstition or deception, than with scientific investigation; yet there is much to learn by the study of even such a common-place phenomenon. The act of writing, when once the habit has been acquired, seems so easy as to be almost intuitive, and we are apt to forget what combinations are necessary to set in motion the pen which runs so glibly over the paper, and what complicated processes are involved in so simple an act. Without dwelling on the mechanism of the hand, it will be enough to call to mind the other requisites for this mode of expression. First, the mental conception, then the volitional impulse and its transmission along the proper track, and then the muscular effort. All this implies a brain capable of originating the idea, and a sound nervous system to carry it out: and any failure in the one or the other mars the execution of the purpose. For instance, certain changes in the brain would alter the modes of expression, showing an incoherency or perversion of idea, or disease in the nervous track might debar a person from expressing the idea really formed and substitute another, or certain muscular defects might impair the execution of the purpose, making the written words shaky or badly formed, &c. So much is self-evident to any one giving the subject any reflection, and these considerations tend to show that the writing of a person may deserve a two-fold study—as to the subject-matter, and the method of execution. From either point of view the writing may, then, have its psychological value, whether a person be sane or insane, and serve as an indication of character, of health, or of disease. Most people are sensible of the force of this indication, though some are far better interpreters of it than others. Writing is, of course, the direct reflection of a person's mind, except in cases where there is a deliberate purpose to mislead or conceal, and from its permanence is sometimes more valuable than the fleeting impression produced by actions or spoken language.

My present object is merely to speak of the value of the study of the writing of the insane, and that in a two-fold aspect; viz., the subject-matter and the manner in which it is conveyed, that is to say, the hand-writing.

There is a popular notion that the insane are a very wily and cunning class, and require to be approached with a certain amount of suspicion and caution, in order to fathom their motives or even discover their weaknesses; but those who live amongst the insane know well how little such notions are supported by facts. The vast majority of the insane, indeed, are unconscious in what way they differ from the rest of the world, and have, therefore, nothing to conceal. Few of them indeed would be able to carry out any system of deception. Still, there are some who will resort to such devices, when they will put a certain constraint on their words and conceal their real thoughts; but this is a difficult part to play, and one that they seldom perform with success. Indeed, most of such patients escape from this unnatural position by relieving their feelings in writing, and then the productions of their pen have an unusual value. Dryden relates of Nathaniel Lee that the latter, in reply to some bad poet, who observed that it was very easy to write like a madman, made this shrewd remark:— *"It is very difficult to write like a madman, but it is very easy to write like a fool."*

It is not necessary that I should here define "the insane," as I only refer to a class recognised as such, and do not want to dwell on any disputed cases. The line must be drawn somewhere between the sane and insane for purposes of public convenience, but such a boundary mark has but little value to medical men, who have to look at people's minds and nervous systems as they are, without much reference to an ideal standard of mental health or capacity. Indeed, the habit of regarding society as divided into two camps, the sane and insane, more or less opposed to one another, is a very mischievous one, as well as being founded in error, for it is those who occupy the neutral ground that it concerns the physician to know, still more than it does those already ticketed as insane. There is a large class of persons, particularly among women, of limited mental capacity, and of unstable nervous power, whose ailments are very closely related to the condition called insanity, and who ought to be studied *clinically* in that category; yet to call such people mad is to unsettle all existing systems of nomenclature. The great majority of cases in any large public Asylum is composed of people who have permanent delusions, or are more or less sunk in dementia; and the mental state of such patients is easily recognised and defined; but there are always a good many others of feeble mind and with little power or will, and without any special perversion of intellect, whose condition hardly differs from the "nervous" and hysterical or susceptible people that exist free in the world. This intermediate class deserves especial study, and forms, as it were, a connecting link between those of vigorous mental health and those whose minds are obviously off the line. But such are just the persons who are the most wearisome patients, and who feed the numerous forms of quackery. The proper way to understand such cases is to think of them as victims of a permanent state, and not objects for pharmaceutical treatment. At all events, the experience of the more aggravated forms of such a state, as seen in the insane, throws the best light on their interpretation.

This is well illustrated by the following extract from a letter I received from the sister of a man who was convalescing from an attack of mania, and wrote to her saying that he wished to see her. This man had been on good terms with her, but had led a wandering life, and had not seen her for some years; he was quiet, and wrote her a sensible letter. In reply she excused herself from doing anything for him, saying—"the principal reason being my own lamentable state of health. I suffer from extreme nervous debility, which renders my daily duties a trial that no one but myself can form the faintest idea of, but which several eminent medical men can and are willing to confirm, should you think it necessary. It would endanger my life (or worse, my reason) if ever I had but an interview with my unfortunate brother. I pray God it may be averted, for only the reading of his letter has completely prostrated me." The inevitable P. S. was as follows:— "I must leave it to your kind consideration to frame an answer to my poor brother for me; it is not in my power to answer him."

This woman, married, and able to attend to her family, partly earned her living by teaching music, though from her letter it might be supposed she was incapable of any exertion. Now, such a state of mind is more nearly allied to insanity than anything else, and some light is thrown on its nature by the fact of her brother being insane. The mere fact of insanity is not enough to deprive a man of the power of writing usefully and serviceably, as is proved by many well-known cases. For instance, A. Cruden, who wrote the "Concordance," had his life interrupted three or four times by attacks of insanity, but left a work behind him which remains of considerable value, Cowper, the poet, too, is another case in point.

J. Clare, the peasant poet of Northamptonshire, was insane for many years, and wrote very good verses while in the Asylum. He had, at that time, various delusions, and would depict with the most minute accuracy the execution of Charles I., of which he professed to have been an eyewitness. He would also describe, in nautical phrase, the battle of the Nile and the death of Nelson, and used to say he was one of his sailors, though he had never seen the sea in his life. These instances show how, even when the mind is permanently affected, men can write on many subjects without giving signs of their infirmities.

It is, however, the exception for those who are permanently insane to be able to carry on any sustained labour in composition.

The letters of the insane are worth study—as the most reliable evidence of the state of the patient^s mind for the time being; they are a sort of involuntary photograph, and for this reason it is often useful to make patients write, as well as to converse with them when investigating cases of lunacy.

I propose to give a few examples of such compositions, and it may be convenient to consider them under the following heads:—

1. As illustrating chronic insanity.
2. As illustrations; acute attacks.
3. As (rarely) the sole evidence.
4. As a sign of convalescence.
5. As indicating an on-coming attack.
6. As illustrating the phases of cases of ordinary mania.
7. As showing the changes the handwriting undergoes in general paralysis.

(1) The following letter was written by a man who was several years under my care, and had permanent delusions. He was a skilful workman, and quiet and well-behaved, but was indignant at what he considered his unjust detention. Before admission to the Asylum, he went to the police to complain of shrieks he

thought he heard from a cellar, and after a time telegraphed to the Duke of Cambridge, which led to his being placed under certificates. Soon after, he wrote a letter describing his arrest, and went on to say—"I have been here about six weeks, and have been tyrannized over the last three months by a set of little devils who call themselves Catholics. They are about 2 feet 6 inches to 4 feet in height; they watched me about London and C.; they parade the fields adjoining this building day and night. I have heard screams from ladies often—all the Princesses of the Royal House are obliged to wander about these fields frequently j if they attempt to get away from these tyrannesses they stop and torture them. Their Highnesses suffer martyrdom from hunger and fatigue, &c. . . . However fabulous or erroneous tnis may appear to some, I assure you it is a fact;—if I could get away from this place, I would go to London and tell you more about these fiends. I have written thus to let you know that the working classes will lose their liberty if they allow this tyranny to exist."

After a time this man found out that his ideas were treated as delusions, and was chary of expressing them, but would betray them when writing a recital of his hardships. I only quote this as a sample of a case of chronic mania, and it has otherwise no special value.

In another case, a woman who was thought by her friends fit to be at liberty wrote thus:—

"I am happy to say that I am in a sound state of mind—but one thing I have to state to you, that there is several wicthes conceiled in this Asiliam, and dockter Backen knows nothing about it; they have been playing on me ever since I have been here—from my hilda

Dutch
Church Ship
America
Jamaica
B

Or Schul
Dear
Fret not thyself
You are in safety
By protection
of his Majesty

Honey Ann Orner
Mr Masterson Bensel note

order
quill
particulars
request, to
be present
Now in

by Chespe
Chateus
near or guechet

Gutta Better pipes to
Bessie Read
punch Bowl
149
Brother at Ward
Boston 2 Thomas St
Boston America

profit and loss
here comes the
tail of the Kite
By the cat
in
the copper

to be taken
care of in
the desk

wave dead
office | hours

toe to my head. What I have suffered, know toung can tell—and I have had a great deal of money sent on here from Weymouth—50 millions, thousand more —and a Hat Box and Box of clothes, and 4 Thousand pounds; besides this, the Queen 50 million Pounds, and the wicked witch here have got it," &c. The woman that wrote this, I may add, had had two husbands, both of whom committed suicide, and after this twofold liberation from the cares of matrimony she became mad herself.

In cases like the two last, diagnosis is easy, but no description can convey so good an idea of the patients' minds as their own expression of their thoughts.

(2) Plate I represents a portion of a letter written by a man during an attack of acute mania. The incoherency of idea, broken purpose, and want of consequence in the words, is shown in the odd scrawl and fantastic figures. It gives a better picture of his mental state than any verbal description could. This letter was addressed "To Her Majesties Most Humble Hannah B., or Mrs. Benja., High St., Ipswich, Clare, Suffolk C, East L.E.C. By Six Mile Bottom. . . . to return unpaid."

This patient was admitted in a state of considerable excitement, and remained for two or three months talkative, unsettled, and incoherent, and with a good deal of emotional excitement. The above letter was written during this stage. By the end of six months he had got much calmer, and was working at his trade, and got better by keeping to a regular employment.

(3) The cases are rare in which patients give no evidence of their insanity, except in writing, but they

do occur. When, however, this is the case, it is only for a time; for, as the symptoms get more confirmed, the mental perversion becomes more intense, and masters the previous resolution to conceal. Not long ago a woman, whose husband was under my care for mental symptoms due to a blow on the head, called to see him, and I was asked to give an opinion as to her sanity, having been furnished with an account of what she had said and done lately. In talking to her, I took great care to avoid exciting her suspicions, but could get nothing from her corroborative of what I had been told, and, indeed, could find nothing wrong with her, though I thought her haggard, and anxious, and altered in appearance. The next day I received the following letter from her:—

"Since I saw you I have made up my mind to go to S. I hope you will believe me that I never was in any way disgracefully connected with any man—I can clear myself, and will; but I feel so completely stunned that I scarcely know what I am after. I feel truly thankful for the kindness shown my poor husband. I will see you again soon, and will then do all I can to set it right." These expressions referred to her delusions, but I had not touched on them in conversation with her. She could not, however, conceal them entirely.

To my surprise I received, a few days later, a second letter, as follows:—

"I was very sorry I was not made acquainted with this affair, so that my poor husband might have had food sufficient—why was it not stated to me in a right way? I beg that he have his proper meals, and what is required for him: it's not right that he should be treated like this. I had no idea for what purpose I was taken there." Shortly after this she was placed in the Asylum, and I found she had a notion that people were talking of her in church and scandalizing her, and interpreted everything she saw as directed at herself. In such case the writing is a powerful aid in diagnosis at an early period, but, of course, where the patient is under daily observation, and her sayings and doings can be noticed by those about her without her knowledge, an opinion is much more easily arrived at. When delusions are active and enter into the patient's being so as to form a part of his daily life and thoughts, he cannot conceal them long; he may do so from the many, but in the end he chooses some confidant.

I knew a gentleman who was for many years in a private asylum, and who mixed daily with a number of persons without betraying himself in the smallest degree, but who would confide to one of the proprietors his thoughts, and who had positive delusions of a distressing character.

(4) I mentioned before that the character of the writing was indicative of the stage in cases of acute mania, and I would observe, in addition, that it often serves to show the progress a patient is making towards recovery. This is well shown in the following letters, which were written by a girl of sixteen, who was under my care last year for a rather sharp attack of acute mania, lasting eight months before entire recovery.

The first letter was written about five months after admission, and was as follows, but badly spelt, &c., as she was uneducated:—

"My dear Father and Mother,—I write these few lines to you, hoping to find you all quite well, as it leaves me at this present time, as I am happy to say it leaves me. Tell Aunt M. I want a new dress for Sunday. I shall not forget the spree we had in the bedroom; we must be silly to think that we was going to leave home for a few weeks, so I shall expect a good long letter from my dear uncle, if he will write to me. I think I know where I am. You did frighten me when I was a-bed, so I shall not forget you. Tell my sister Mary to write to me, for I shall be glad to hear from her. Brother J. came to see me a few days back. I hope he is well, and dear Mother as well, &c. I want my petticoat from B. Tell my dear uncle to send me my things, as I am so happy to see the parlour fire burn so fierce. Give my love to all my old fellow-servants. I hope you will forgive me, uncle, for waiting of you, so you must go home and wait table for Mr. B., squire at Hall, and get me saddling ready for hunting, but you must not forget Mary and me. I want to go to D. with you for a ride in the dog-cart, and feed the cats up the loft. Don't forget the whip and horse-rug to go to. My kindest ove to them all, and receive the same yourself; you know me, I suppose," &c.

The next letter she wrote, to her parents also, was this:—

"I write these few lines, hoping to find you all well, as it leaves all of us. I didn't write to you before because I was waiting to get well, to come home. It is very cold in the summer time. Tell Sister Mary to please to write to me before I leave off working; it is time to have a letter from you. I think I shall work to-morrow, so please give my kind love to all friends. I did not think of seeing Aunt O.; so coming in to see, she was dead and buried," &c.

The third letter was written two months before her discharge from the Asylum, thus:—

"I write these few lines," &c., &c. "It is very wet and cold. There is a very nice fire here this afternoon. I have been expecting some of you to see me for this last fortnight. I go to the dance every time; I enjoy myself very much. I am getting quite well now, I shall soon be fit to come home again. They are all very kind to me here. Give my love to all my brothers and sisters," &c.

These letters, though simple, deserve consideration, as showing the variations in the mental state. This girl had been staying with an uncle, who was servant to a gentleman in Yorkshire, and the first letter is a curious jumble of home impressions and feelings, with reminiscences of her visit to her uncle, and the details of her life there, such as the stables, the cats, and the ride in the dog-cart. The next letter shows a great improvement, but there is still some flightiness; and the last is quite sensible in tone.

Such a series of letters is useful, as showing the gradual improvement in a case, and assists one in forming an opinion on its progress.

(5) An anxiety to write is frequently the sign of an ap-proaching attack. A woman, who has been some time under my care, for recurrent mania, always takes to her pen at the onset of an attack. She writes letters, and crosses them, fills up every corner of the paper, and, when finished, they are quite unintelligible, and consist mostly of a repetition of the same sentences. In such a case the writing is superfluous for a medical man, so far as diagnosis is concerned, but it might be useful in convincing others, as loquacious females,

who have no absurd delusions, are very apt to be regarded by the public as sane, and only injured and misunderstood creatures.

(6) In ordinary cases of mania the patients' letters are odd and grotesque, exhibiting the same want of balance that their actions do. These productions are of little value in diagnosis, but are curious illustrations of the topsy-turvy condition of the writer's mind. This is well illustrated in the following case:—The patient was a respectable artisan of considerable intelligence, and was sent to the Cambridgeshire Asylum after being nearly three years in a melancholy mood. As this passed off, he showed a good deal of pride and self-esteem, and gradually recovered, so that at the end of two years more he was able to be discharged. During the greater part of these two years he spent much of his time in writing—sometimes verses, at others long letters of the most rambling character, and in drawing extraordinary diagrams, of which the coloured illustrations (the frontispiece and Plate III) present striking instances. They are not quite so incomprehensible as they at first appear, for on close inspection a good many ideas may be made out. After he left the Asylum he went to work at his trade, and, by steady application, succeeded in arriving at a certain degree of prosperity, but some two or three years later he began to write very strangely again, and had some of his odd productions printed; yet all this time he kept at work, earned plenty of money, conducted his business very sensibly, and would converse reasonably.

This is one of the letters he wrote at this time, after a visit from a medical man, who tried to dissuade him from writing in this way:—

"Dear Doctor,

"To write or not to write, that is the question. Whether 'tis nobler in the mind to follow the visit of the great 'Fulbourn' with 'chronic melancholy' expressions of regret (withheld when he was here) that, as the Fates would have it, we were so little prepared to receive him, and to evince my humble desire to do honour to his visit. My Fulbourn star, but an instant seen, like a meteor's flash, a blank when gone.

"The dust of ages covering my little sanctum parlour room, the available drapery to greet the Doctor, stowed away through the midst of the regenerating (water and scrubbing—cleanliness next to godliness, political and spiritual) cleansing of a little world. The Great Physician walked, bedimmed by the 'dark ages,' the long passage of Western Enterprise, leading to the curvatures of rising Eastern morn. The rounded configuration of Lunar (tics) garden's lives an o'ershadowment on Britannia's vortex" &c.

The coloured illustration facing the Title-page is another of his strange productions. It would require no little ingenuity to conceive, and perseverance to execute, such a diagram, and the curious feature in the case is, that a man with such disordered ideas should concentrate his efforts sufficiently for such an undertaking. His industry in composition and the odd illustrations by which he accompanied his writings, were marvellous, and on the whole his case was a very extraordinary one.

The illustration in Plate III and that forming the frontispiece were, in the original, drawn on both sides of the same small half sheet of paper, and the patient,

HIGHLY FAVOUR-ED

WHEN THE MORNING STARS SANG TOGETHER AND ALL THE SONS OF GOD SHOUTED FOR JOY

COMMANDED THE MORNING

COMING FROM AFAR

UNIVERSAL KEY

MAGNETISM

KETTLE

THE ALMIGHTY

as though anxious, in the exuberance of his fancy, to make the fullest use of his opportunities, had filled up every morsel of the surface—to the very edge—not leaving an atom of margin. On looking at it one is strikingly reminded of the lines in Pope's Essay on Man—

> "A mighty maze! but not without a plan,
> A wild, where weeds and flowers promiscuous shoot;"

although it may not be easy to find the key to this plan, whatever it might have been, nor to distinguish which are the weeds and which the flowers in so tangled a "wild."

In the course of another year he had some domestic troubles, which upset him a good deal, and he ended by drowning himself one day in a public spot. The peculiarity was, that he could work well, and not attract public attention, while he was in his leisure moments writing the most incoherent nonsense.

Another case I had under my care recently, showed some strange peculiarities in this direction. The patient had been of unsteady habits, and reduced himself to poverty, and was sent to the Asylum with certain delusions as to the Jews, and an army he had at his command. After a time he disowned his wife, and refused to communicate with her, but later wrote the letter of which Plate II is a facsimile. That in printed capitals he called the Italian version, and the other the Key to it. He recovered completely in eleven months, but his symptoms underwent several changes before he left, and his letters varied with them. After the letter just referred to, he wrote one with every second or third word in capitals, the subject-matter being quite incoherent. Shortly afterwards he wrote two more, composed wholly of unmeaning marks and strokes, of which he gave no explanation. When he approached recovery he wrote very sensibly and affectionately to his wife, showing genuine remorse for his bad habits, and was also full of good intentions, which I believe were carried out.

The cases which the public cannot understand, and which often furnish sensational instances, are chiefly those in which no obvious delusions exist. When a man can answer a few simple questions correctly, and talk of his being unjustly detained in an Asylum, many people are apt to say that he has no "*insanity*" about him, but all the while he may be so deficient in will or self-control, or the energy that is necessary to direct the actions, that he is quite unfit to manage himself or hold his own in the world. I have for the last three years had under my care a case which illustrates this well. The patient is a young man who has been respectably brought up, and had some little property. He had tried some occupation, and was for a few weeks a clerk in a bank, but left it. He then lived with an aunt, and had no employment. In consequence of some extravagancies of conduct he was placed in the Asylum, and soon settled down comfortably. His hours were spent in fussy idleness, though he talked as if his time were so filled up he could not undertake anything: he had also several silly projects. He was always writing letters, sending for catalogues which were advertised gratis, almanacks, shilling books, &c., and ordering various things without any idea of paying for them, but was quite unaware of the inconsistency of his conduct. After a time he wanted an estate, was very anx-

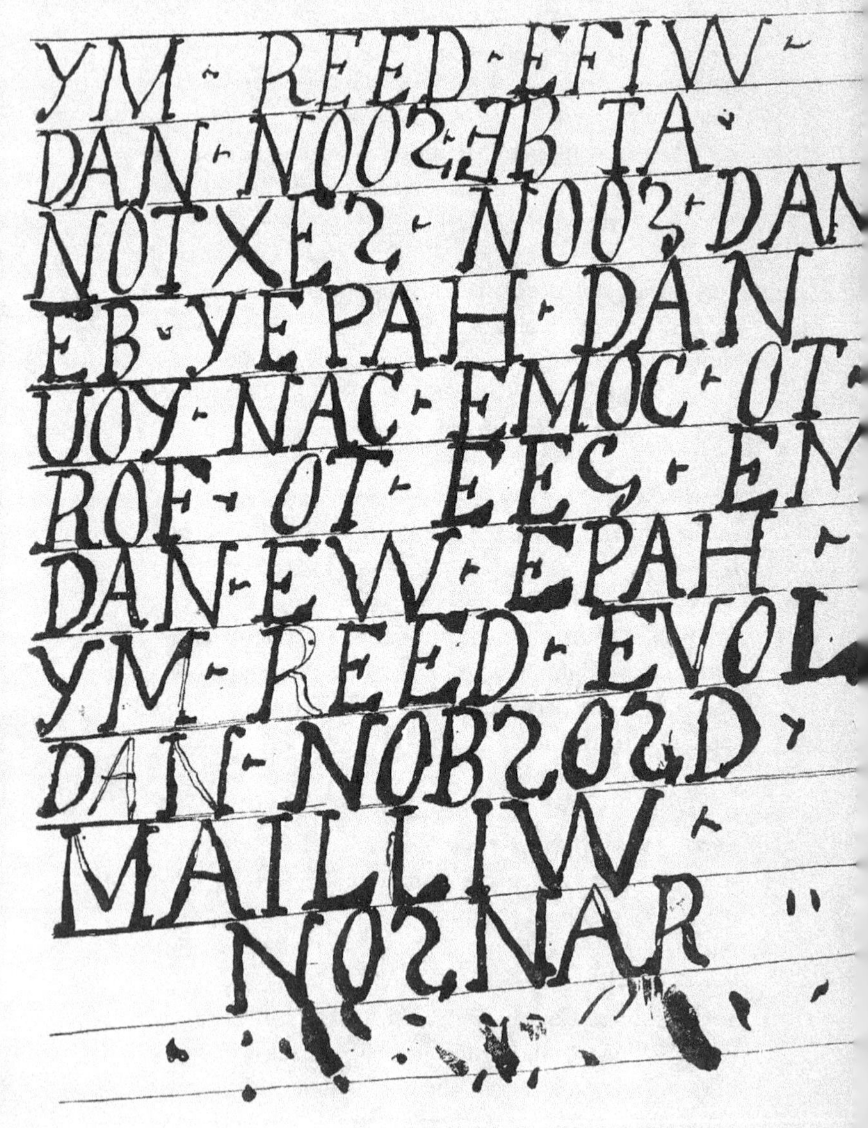
YM REED EFIW
DAN NOOS EB TA
NOTXES NOOS DAN
EB YEPAH DAN
UOY NAC EMOC OT
ROF OT EES EM
DAN EW EPAH
YM REED EVOL
DAN NOBSOSD
MAILLIW
NOSNAR

My Deer Wife
I am hapey and
to shall see at
Filet at sexton
and you can come
and see me from
your Lowen hasten
William Roberd Ranson

ious to get married, and proposed to build a church on Lundy Island. Now this man's ordinary conversation showed none of the absurd ideas that are expected as signs of insanity, but his conduct, taken as a whole, was proof of the real state of his mind. Had he been rich, and made the subject of a Lunacy Commission, probably the jury which found Mr. Windham not insane would have given this man a similar verdict. His letters, generally, were very amusing, and showed the condition of his mind. On one occasion he wrote to a London tradesman for specimens of dies and paper, &c., and his letter was sent back to me as unintelligible. It was as follows:—

"F. M. R. returns his best thanks and desires to acknowledge the safe receipt of the letter containing the monographic devices, and if Messrs. P. will have the die cut, in nice, exact style, and 500 medium envelopes, half ream of paper, &c. it will much oblige. If in the event of my not paying the entire order at once, you will obligingly give me credit, and this you need not fear to do. I much wish in the centre of the seal to have a light-house represented, as I wish so much to be enabled erecting one on the Channel side of the Devonshire coast," &c.

"P. S. Should a G. use black wax?"

"One incident, which I may term the second striking one, transpired yesterday. I was just intending to seal the letter; I had no vesta matches by me, consequently left my writing desk and proceeded into the next ward, where, quite unexpectedly to me, a patient had departed this life, and was laid out. With respect to the seal, let it be," &c., &c.

An ordinary stranger might converse for some

time with such a patient as this without getting any answer which would be inconsistent with sanity, but the above letter would convince anybody.

(7) There is one condition in which the character of the handwriting may be of great assistance in diagnosis, viz., the disease commonly known as "general paralysis." I mean by this term the disease characterised chiefly by the existence of delusions of an extravagant nature at first, and followed by paralysis and general enfeeblement of the limbs and complete dementia, running an average course of three or four years, and always ending fatally; a disease well known in every public asylum, but not at all so clearly recognised out of doors. In this disease, the early symptoms creep on insidiously, and are often only an exaggeration of the ordinary habits of thought and action of certain over-confident and pushing individuals; so that in most cases, people are deceived as to what is really going on. It is, however, in the early stages that the recognition of this disease is important, for after a certain period, when the physical symptoms declare themselves, the diagnosis is easy enough; and it is in the first course of the malady that it is needful to interfere. It is a malady from which the richer classes, and those actively engaged in the excitement of speculation, or the harass of commercial life, particularly suffer, and at the commencement patients are prone to squander their money and commit numerous extravagancies which affect the interests of others. This is the time when friends should interfere to save the needless waste of property, and often to control the actions of the individual, and it is then that the medical man is consulted, but it is seldom that the latter likes to incur

the risk or odium of considering the patient as insane at this stage; he prefers waiting till the extravagancies become more pronounced, or the physical weakness shows more clearly the nature of the disease.

Now, any fact that would tend to facilitate the early determination of such cases is of great value, and I wish to direct attention to the aid that may be derived from studying the handwriting under these circumstances. It is easily seen that, in a progressive disease, attended by increasing muscular weakness, the character of the writing must change; but I do not think that attention has been generally drawn to what I might call the *progressive degeneration* of the writing in this disease. Now, I do not hesitate to say that, excluding local disease, which might impair the power of writing, and setting aside also the mere effects of age, there is no other known disease which alters the handwriting in the peculiar way this is modified by what is called general paralysis of the insane.

If this be true, the study of the writing of such patients at once assumes a fresh importance. The accompanying figures show the extreme changes that occur; but the point to be remembered is this—that if such changes are the natural result of a certain period of this disease, how important it is to be on the alert for the minor alterations which occur earlier.

Fig. 1 (plate 4) is the writing of a gentleman who has died from general paralysis. This is an example of his writing in comparative health, and it was a bold, vigorous style.

Fig. 2 (plate 4) is the writing of the same person only a few months later; but how changed! What strikes an observer in this, is the irregularity, the *shak-*

iness, and the disconnection of the letters. The contrast between Fig, 1 and 2 is as well marked as can be imagined, but there must have been a time when 2% the alteration began to be perceptible, and that was the period when such observation would have been of value. In forming an opinion, it is, of course, necessary to be acquainted with the patient's writing in health, and also to consider his age, and then the comparison of the writing in health and in disease becomes of great value. This indication, too, is of far greater service among the rich and educated than among the poorer classes, who seldom have a distinctive style of their own, and who are unpractised in the art.

Figs. 3 and 4 (plate 4) illustrate the writing of a man in an humble sphere, who was under my care for the mania of general paralysis.

Fig. 4 (plate 4) is his writing in health; and there is a vigour in the words "July" and "Paid," which contrasts strongly with the words in Fig. 3.

Fig. 3 (plate 4) is a fac-simile of his writing soon after his admission. At that time I diagnosed general paralysis, but it was in an early stage, and as the muscular symptoms were not far developed, the case was not one recognised by all as such. The subsequent course, however, quite confirmed my opinion. The last two lines are characteristic examples of the writing of such patients. I would suggest that, with these instances before us, we cannot refuse the conclusion that the writing of general paralytics is, in a certain stage, distinctive; that, excluding certain local conditions, there is nothing else that produces such a gradual and decided change; and that, recognising this *progressive degradation* as a consequence of this disease, it is well to watch for the earliest indications of such change as a material aid in diagnosis.

APPENDIX.

In the position I occupy I receive a good many letters from the poorer class, and have often had from some of my correspondents very odd specimens. The three following are from individuals belonging to what is called the sane portion of the public. In No. 1 the contrast between T. R.'s style and those in the preceding pages is perhaps not so well marked as one would like to expect.

No. 1.

This is from a man whose wife was in the Asylum, but not well enough to leave; she subsequently recovered perfectly.

"Sir,—i have takeing the Liboty to ask you if you will let my Wife come out if i come with her cloths, i have paid up to saterdy night, and was forced to rob a man of his wages to pay you. i paid all i could get before, and then handed out of the room: so now I have declined paying any mor; if you will keep her you must keep her on your own money, for i have no more without Robery, and i cannot do that as the laws are against it here.

"please to right so that i have it on Friday morning

if you will or not; if you will not right let my wife right so that i have it, but not force her to say no: if you let her come out you never shall be plagued with her any more with my consent, if you could not keep her for 9 shilling a week you ought to have sent her home and i would have tryed. i might have had a shirt washed for that other shilling.

"From T. R."

No. 2.

This is from a person I never saw, to whom formal notice of his father's death was sent from the Asylum:—

"deaier Frend gest a line or tue ine answer to youer leter of the deth of Farther and i ame sorey to say that we are poore peepel, so we canot Bee the expence of taken the Bodey away to Bee Bered so it must aboide healer ware we was aBell to have it home we would. But we canot, and if please god some of us will Bee at the silam on Friday morning, our kind reespects to all."

No. 3.

"Respective Sir,

"I right to Inform you that I received your Letter, and was truly thankful to you for your truble and Likewise for you kind attension to my dear diseased wife, and If all is well I shall be thair on Monday, and respection a poste mortal examanation I am quite agreable. If it wod be conveneant I shod like her to be Interd about 12.

"Yrs, &c., J. K."

Among letters addressed to me I have received the following versions of the words "Fulbourn Asylum:"—

"Fulbon asulam,"	"Fullbun Asilom."
"Fulham Esylum."	"Foolbun Asilium."
"Fulbuon asyllum."	"Fullem Asilem."
"Fulborn Asalym."	

The ingenuity in error displayed here is curious.

HANDWRITTEN NOTES

HANDWRITTEN NOTES

REPORT OF THE MEDICAL SUPERINTENDENT

FOR THE YEAR 1880

Report of the Medical Superintendent

FOR THE YEAR 1880.

To the Committee of Visitors

JANUARY, 1881.

The close of the past year found this Asylum with 335 patients, of whom 155 were males and 180 females.

During the year nine male and seventeen female patients were discharged recovered, while fourteen males and eighteen females died in the same period. The list of cures contains one case of special interest—that of a man whose recovery was apparently due to a surgical operation of some importance. The patient had received an injury to his head about eighteen months before his admission, and was sent here after a serious attempt at suicide. About ten weeks after his admission he was trephined at the seat of injury. One month later he was at work in the carpenter's shop, and was discharged quite well, and has remained so, and been able to work at his trade since. The operation was performed by Mr. Geo. E. WHERRY, of Cambridge. This case is published in detail in the

Journal of Mental Science for January, 1881.

In another case the aid of surgical science was equally beneficial to the body, though not to the mind, of the patient, a man who had been for several years in the Asylum, an was suffering from a very large hernia, which could not be kept up by any devices, and which was a source of great trouble and suffering to the patient. In this case Mr. WHERRY performed Wood's operation for the radical cure of hernia. It was done antiseptically. The patient was 60 years of age. Although there were many difficulties in the treatment of the case and the management of the patient, the result was thoroughly successful, and the man can now get about with perfect comfort and is very grateful for the relief afforded him by the procedure.

The Coroner held two inquests in the year, one being on a male patient who died from rupture of the jejunum, produced during a struggle with some of the attendants. The matter was fully inquired into, but the Coroner and jury exonerated the attendants from any blame as to the occurrence. The patient was a very dangerous epileptic, liable to fits of excitement, during which he became very violent, and had been specially watched for some years all day. Besides the mischief he had done to doors, windows, and furniture on various occasions, he had assaulted several of the other patients from time to time. One patient lost an eye from his violence, and another had the lobe of his ear bitten off by him. On the last occasion he was struggling with four attendants, who do not appear to have used unnecessary force or intentional violence towards the patient in removing him to his own room.

The second inquest was held to comply with the law rather than to pursue any investigation. A female patient, aged 50, was pushed off a seat in a day-room by another patient, 80 years of age, and broke her leg in the fall. In consequence of her death about three weeks afterwards, the Coroner felt bound to hold an inquest, when a verdict was returned to the effect that the deceased met with her death "casually, accidentally, and not otherwise."

A *post-mortem* examination showed that the patient was in a very diseased condition. She had fatty disease of the heart, double pneumonia, cystitis, ovarian cysts, her ribs were soft and broke under slight pressure, and the bones generally were in a pathological state of fragility.

Another of the deaths deserves record, as the case was very unusual. A woman lived to the age of 53, having been hydrocephalic since an early age. She was admitted into the Asylum in 1871, and died in 1880. Her head measured 27 inches in circumference. The skull was completely ossified, and unusually dense in places. Notwithstanding her infirmities, she had considerable intelligence, had fair memory, could sing, repeat hymns, &c., sew a little, and converse. As regards the size of the head, her case has not many equals, and it is, I believe, very unusual for hydrocephalics to attain such an age as this patient had.

One of the female patients was admitted in a pregnant state, and was confined in October.

The staff of the Asylum has suffered from the vicissitudes of life, to which flesh is heir in an unusual degree, during the last year. Mr. PARISH, who had acted as Chaplain to the Asylum since its opening in 1858, resigned and left at Michaelmas last, being promoted to a more fortunate career elsewhere. He carried with him the good wishes and regrets of all who knew him. He was always regarded as a welcome friend by all, ever ready to sympathise with and assist those that were sick or sorrowing, and in an unobstrusive manner fulfilling his duties in a kindly and efficient way.

The Porter (CHEVERTON) has been suffering from illness a great part of the year; he has also been much missed, not only on account of his own good and useful qualities, but by reason of his long association with the Asylum. He was the first servant engaged, and was in office previous to the opening of the Asylum in November, 1858.

Another old servant, Samuel Wright, who had been for nearly 20 years employed here, chiefly as Night Attendant, left during the year, having migrated to another county. These changes have not been without sensible effect on many of the inhabitants of the place, but, on the other hand, it is only right to acknowledge, and with welcome, the recent addition to the staff of an Assistant Medical Officer-Mr. R. J. BOYD. This gentleman has shown great energy and interest in his work, and I gladly acknowledge his services as my colleague. With his help, I trust the management of the Asylum may be conducted more profitably and satisfactorily than was possible before, considering the number of patients and extent of the establishment.

The usual statistical tables are appended, but they require a note of caution to those who may care to study them. In my last annual report I referred to certain disturbing causes which affected the value of these statistics, and foretold the same danger for the next year's issue. I must repeat it now, and again explain that the admissions and discharges are largely affected by the removal of some 40 male patients in the last year, while the buildings were being enlarged, and by the re-admission of most of the same men before the close of 1880. These cases figure among the "relapsed" cases in the table, and the "Not Improved" in the Discharges. But they are not "relapsed" and only "re-admitted" cases. Again, "re-admission" means practically the recurrence of an attack in a previously cured patient, but in these cases it means nothing of the sort, and so may mislead those who deal with these calculations. It is obvious also that the percentage of cures on admissions is seriously affected by the inclusion of these re-admissions, as about four-fifths of the male admissions for 1880 were incurable at starting, and not an ordinary sample of the cases admitted into Asylums in the usual course of events. To avoid these errors there is wanted, it seems to me, a separate column of "transfers," distinguished from the regular ad missions, such as that which occurs in the Lunacy Commissioners' annual return. I have also added a note to table 1, in the hope of elucidating the question of real recoveries, by recording the number of attacks that individual patients have passed through, as well as *cases* that have been admitted. The figures only apply to the past year, but I hope, on another occasion, to tabulate all the admissions since the opening of the Asylum, and by this means carry out the plan suggested by Dr. HACK TUKE, and ascertain the number of *persons* cured.

I feel it is only by such a method that we can arrive at the knowledge of what cases are really cured, and that it is important that Asylum Superintendents should know how many patients recover, in the sense of being restored to health for at least a considerable period, and not merely how soon a recovered patient returns to the same Asylum to again go through the farce of a recovery, and be re-admitted perhaps in a week or a month.

G. MACKENZIE BACON, M.A., M.D.

TABLE I.

Showing the Admissions, Re-Admissions, Discharges, and Deaths during the Year 1880.

				Male.	Female.	Total.
In Asylum, 1st January, 1881				164	176	340
	Male.	Female.	Total.			
Admitted for the first time during the year 1880..	19	38	57			
Re-admitted during the year ..	32	4	36			
Total admitted				51	42	93
Total under care during the year				215	218	433
Discharged or Removed:						
	Male.	Female.	Total.			
Recovered	9	17	26			
Relieved	1	2	3			
Not Improved ..	36	1	37			
Died	14	18	32			
Total discharged and died during the year				60	38	98
Remaining in the Asylum, Dec. 31st, 1880				155	180	335
Average number resident during the year				134	177	311

Note.—Of the female re-admissions two cases were treated for a second attack, one for a third, and one for a fourth. All the other cases were merely transfers of chronic cases.

TABLE II.

Showing the Admissions, Re-admissions, and Discharges, from the opening of the Asylum, to the present date, Dec. 31st., 1880.

	Male.	Female.	Total.
Persons admitted during the period of 22 years and more, that is, since Nov. 2nd, 1858	836	932	1768
Re-admissions	131	162	293
Total of Cases admitted	967	1094	2061
Discharged or removed:			

	Male.	Female.	Total.
Recovered	307	415	789
Relieved	78	81	159
Not improved ..	73	73	146
Died	354	345	699

	Male.	Female.	Total.
Total discharged and died during the 22 years and more	812	914	1726
Remaining, Dec. 31st, 1880	155	180	335
Average number resident during the 22 years	130	147	277

TABLE III.

Showing the Admissions, Discharges, and Deaths, with the mean annual Mortality and Proportion of Recoveries per cent. of the Admissions for each year since the opening of the Asylum.

Year.	Admitted.			Discharged. Recovered.			Discharged. Relieved.			Discharged. Not Improved.			Died.			Remaining 31st Dec. in each year.			Average No. Resident.			Per centage of Recoveries on Admissions.			Per centage of Deaths on average No. Resident.		
	Male.	Female.	Total.	Male.	Female.	Total.	Male.	Female.	Total.	Male.	Female.	Total.	Male.	Female.	Total.	Male.	Female.	Total.	Male.	Female.	Total.	Male.	Female.	Total.	Male.	Female.	Total.
1858..	60	58	118	..	1	1	..	..	..	..	..	..	2	1	3	59	56	115	45	45	90	..	1·7	·8	2·2	2·2	2·2
1859..	40	37	77	14	12	26	2	..	2	1	..	1	7	3	10	74	78	152	73	74	147	35·	32·4	33·7	9·5	40·5	6·8
1860..	40	59	99	5	17	22	4	1	5	..	..	..	18	9	27	87	110	197	82	96	178	12·5	28·8	22·2	21·9	9·3	15·1
1861..	59	67	126	14	29	43	2	1	3	4	1	5	17	11	28	109	135	244	96	131	227	22·3	43·2	34·1	17·7	8·3	12·3
1862..	47	44	91	15	22	37	3	2	5	..	1	1	15	12	27	123	142	265	116	138	254	31·9	50·	40·6	12·9	8·6	10·6
1863..	45	46	91	16	18	34	4	1	5	2	..	2	14	17	31	133	152	285	130	148	278	35·5	39·1	37·3	10·7	11·4	11·1
1864..	39	43	82	16	17	33	4	18	22	..	3	3	16	9	25	136	148	284	137	151	288	41·	39·5	40·2	11·6	5·9	8·6
1865..	42	47	89	20	20	40	2	3	5	..	..	..	16	13	29	140	159	299	136	152	288	47·6	42·5	44·9	11·7	9·5	10·6
1866..	40	50	90	10	24	34	10	8	18	8	16	24	18	15	33	133	146	279	144	162	306	25·	48·	37·7	12·5	9·2	10·7
1867..	30	45	75	17	25	42	7	1	8	..	..	..	11	20	31	128	145	273	126	146	272	56·6	55·5	56·	8.7	13·6	11·3
1868..	40	48	88	14	19	33	1	6	7	4	2	6	15	10	25	134	156	290	135	149	284	35·	39·5	37·5	11·1	6·7	8·8
1869..	30	45	75	13	16	29	3	2	5	1	8	9	21	27	48	126	148	274	133	158	291	43·3	35·5	38·6	15·7	17·	16·4
1870..	38	43	81	11	22	33	18	13	31	2	..	2	11	11	22	122	145	267	128	149	277	28·9	51·1	40·7	8·5	7·3	8·3
1871..	38	29	67	17	16	33	1	6	7	1	..	1	16	16	32	125	136	261	125	138	263	44·7	55·1	49·2	12·8	11·5	12·1
1872..	33	45	78	15	18	33	3	2	5	2	..	2	13	14	27	125	147	272	123	143	266	45·4	40·	42·3	10·5	9·7	10·1
1873..	30	38	68	14	17	31	..	..	..	..	2	2	16	18	34	125	148	273	127	150	277	46·2	44·7	55·5	12·4	12·	12·2
1874..	41	38	79	9	17	26	..	1	1	1	1	2	14	14	28	142	153	295	133	153	286	21·9	44·7	32·9	10·5	9·1	9·7
1875..	43	52	95	27	18	45	5	5	10	..	..	..	25	29	54	128	153	281	130	150	280	62·7	34·6	47·8	19·2	19·3	19·2
1876..	54	46	100	14	15	29	1	4	5	3	2	5	14	20	34	150	158	308	140	157	297	25·9	32·6	29·	10·	12·7	11·4
1877..	42	50	92	18	12	30	4	2	6	2	1	3	23	25	48	145	168	313	148	161	309	42·8	24·6	35·8	15·5	15·5	15·5
1878..	49	68	117	13	24	37	1	1	2	2	35	37	16	20	36	162	156	318	155	155	310	26·7	35·2	31·6	10·3	13·9	11·6
1879..	36	54	90	6	19	25	2	2	4	4	0	4	22	13	35	164	176	340	161	165	326	16·6	35·8	27·7	13·6	7·8	10·7
1880..	51	42	93	9	17	26	1	2	3	36	1	37	14	18	32	155	180	335	134	177	311	17·6	40·4	27·9	10·4	10·1	10·2
Total..	967	1094	2061	307	415	722	78	81	159	73	73	146	354	345	699	..	..	..	..	..	..	..	..	..	..	..	..

TABLE IV.

Showing the History of the Annual Admissions since the opening of the Asylum, with the Discharges and Deaths and the Numbers of each Year remaining on the 31st December, 1880.

	Admitted.					Of each Year's Admissions Discharged and Died in 1880.												Total Discharged and Died of each Year's Admissions to 31st December, 1880.												Remaining of each Year's Admissions, 31 Dec., 1880.		
	New Cases.		Relapsed Cases			Recovered.			Relieved.			Not Improved.			Died.			Recovered.			Relieved.			Not Improved.			Died.					
YEAR.	Male.	Female.	Male.	Female.	Total.	Male.	Female.	Total.	Male.	Female.	Total.	Male.	Female.	Total.	Male.	Female.	Total.	Male.	Female.	Total.	Male.	Female.	Total.	Male.	Female.	Total.	Male.	Female.	Total.	Male.	Female.	Total.
1858..	60	58	..	..	118	..	..	..	..	..	..	5	..	5	1	..	1	4	9	13	2	..	2	5	2	7	36	38	74	13	9	22
1859..	39	37	1	..	77	..	..	..	..	..	..	..	..	..	..	..	..	11	20	31	4	3	7	1	..		17	12	29	4	2	6
1860..	35	57	5	2	99	..	..	..	..	..	..	1	..	1	..	..	..	9	21	30	7	12	19	5	7	12	16	18	34	1	1	2
1861..	55	60	4	7	126	..	..	..	..	..	..	2	..	2	..	..	..	18	31	49	6	10	16	6	12	18	25	11	36	4	3	7
1862..	41	42	6	2	91	..	..	..	..	..	..	..	..	..	..	..	..	17	14	31	5	5	10	2	3	5	18	18	36	5	4	9
1863..	41	42	4	4	91	..	..	..	..	..	..	..	..	..	..	..	..	14	19	33	4	4	8	3	2	5	22	18	40	2	3	5
1864..	37	38	2	5	82	..	..	..	..	..	..	1	..	1	..	..	..	16	18	34	7	7	14	1	1	2	13	16	29	2	1	3
1865..	38	43	4	4	89	..	..	..	..	..	..	..	..	..	1	..	1	16	24	40	6	3	9	1	5	6	14	12	26	5	3	8
1866..	38	42	2	8	90	..	..	..	..	..	..	..	..	..	1	..	1	12	20	32	7	4	11	4	2	6	14	21	35	3	3	6
1867..	25	36	5	9	75	..	..	..	..	..	..	..	..	..	..	..	..	15	24	39	4	2	6	..	4	4	10	9	19	1	6	7
1868..	33	36	7	12	88	..	..	..	..	..	..	2	..	2	..	..	..	15	16	31	3	5	8	5	1	6	17	21	38	..	5	5
1869..	27	36	3	9	75	..	..	..	..	..	..	..	..	..	..	..	..	10	23	33	4	2	6	1	1	2	14	10	24	1	9	10
1870..	33	30	5	13	81	..	..	..	..	..	..	..	..	..	1	..	1	15	18	33	3	4	7	1	2	3	12	15	27	7	4	11
1871..	30	18	8	11	67	..	..	..	..	..	..	..	..	..	2	2	4	19	14	33	..	2	2	2	1	3	12	9	21	5	3	8
1872..	26	41	7	4	78	..	..	..	..	..	..	1	..	1	..	1	1	13	16	29	2	1	3	2	4	6	13	18	31	3	6	9
1873..	23	27	7	11	68	..	..	..	..	..	..	4	..	4	..	..	..	9	12	21	..	1	1	4	6	10	13	15	28	4	4	8
1874..	36	35	5	3	79	..	..	..	..	..	..	3	..	3	1	..	1	16	17	33	4	3	7	3	1	4	16	14	30	2	3	5
1875..	39	45	4	7	95	..	..	..	..	..	..	2	..	2	..	..	..	18	18	36	2	3	5	3	3	6	15	18	33	5	10	15
1876..	48	44	6	2	100	..	..	..	..	..	..	2	1	3	..	2	2	17	16	33	3	5	8	3	7	10	19	13	32	12	5	17
1877..	37	43	5	7	92	..	..	..	..	..	..	2	..	2	2	..	2	18	13	31	1	..	1	4	8	12	13	15	28	6	14	20
1878..	42	46	7	22	117	..	2	2	..	..	..	3	..	3	1	4	5	10	28	38	2	2	4	7	1	8	14	13	27	16	24	40
1879..	34	38	2	16	90	3	6	9	1	..	1	7	..	7	3	5	8	6	15	21	2	1	3	9	..	9	10	7	17	9	31	40
1880..	19	38	32	4	93	6	9	15	..	2	2	1	..	1	1	4	5	6	9	15	..	2	2	1	..	1	1	4	5	43	27	70
Total..	836	932	131	162	2061	9	17	26	1	2	3	36	1	37	14	18	32	307	415	722	78	81	159	73	73	156	354	345	699	155	180	335

TABLE V.

Showing the causes of Death during the Year.

Cause of Death.	Male.	Female.	Total.
Cerebral or Spinal Disease.			
Apoplexy and Paralysis	..	..	..
Epilepsy and Convulsions	..	..	..
General Paralysis	1	3	4
Maniacal and Melancholic Exhaustion or Decay	..	..	..
Inflammation and other Diseases of the Brain, Softening, Tumours, &c.	2	2	4
Cerebellar Tumour	1	..	1
Thoracic Disease.			
Inflammation of the Lungs, Pleuræ and Bronchi	2	2	4
Pulmonary Consumption	5	4	9
Disease of the Heart	1	1	2
Abdominal Disease.			
Chronic Peritonitis	..	1	1
Ruptured Intestine	1	..	1
Cancer of Stomach	..	1	1
Cancer of Uterus	..	1	1
Cancer of Breast	..	1	1
General Debility and Old Age	1	2	3
Total	14	18	32

TABLE VI.

Showing the length of Residence of those Discharged Recovered, and in those who have Died during the year 1880.

Length of Residence.	Recovered.			Died.		
	Male.	Female.	Total.	Male.	Female.	Total.
Under 1 month	2	..	2	1	1	2
From 1 to 3 months	2	9	11	..	..	..
,, 3 ,, 6 ,, ...	2	3	5	2	2	4
,, 6 ,, 9 ,, ...	2	2	4	..	3	3
,, 9 ,, 12 ,, ...	..	1	1	..	1	1
,, 1 ,, 2 years	1	2	3	2	4	6
,, 2 ,, 3 ,, ...	..	..	..	2	2	4
,, 3 ,, 5 ,, ...	..	..	..	..	2	2
,, 5 ,, 7 ,, ...	..	..	..	1	..	1
,, 7 ,, 10 ,, ...	..	..	..	3	3	6
,, 10 and more.............	..	..	..	3	..	3
Total......	9	17	26	14	18	32

TABLE VII.

Showing the Duration of the Disorder on Admission in the Admissions, Discharges, and Deaths during the Year 1880.

Class.	Duration of Disease on Admission in Four Classes.											
	The Admissions.			The Discharges.						The Deaths.		
				Recovered.			Removed (Relieved or otherwise).					
	Male.	Female.	Total.	Male.	Female.	Total.	Male.	Female.	Total.	Male.	Female.	Total.
FIRST CLASS— First attack, and within three months on admission	8	18	26	7	10	17	6	2	8	3	7	10
SECOND CLASS— First attack, above three and within twelve months on admission	4	5	9	..	2	2	5	1	6	3	4	7
THIRD CLASS— Not first attack, and within twelve months on admission	7	8	15	1	4	5	6	..	6	1	1	2
FOURTH CLASS— First attack or not, but of more than twelve months on admission	31	11	42	1	1	2	17	..	17	7	5	12
Not ascertained	1	..	1	..	..	..	3	..	3	..	1	1
Total..........	51	42	93	9	17	26	37	3	40	14	18	32

TABLE VIII.

Showing the Ages of the Admissions, Discharges, and Deaths during the Year 1880.

Ages.	The Admissions.			The Discharges. Recovered.			The Discharges. Removed (Reliev-ed or otherwise).			The Deaths.		
	Male.	Female.	Total.	Male.	Female.	Total.	Male.	Female.	Total.	Male.	Female.	Total.
From 5 to 10 years	..	..	..	..	..	..	..	..	..	..	..	..
,, 10 15 ,, ...	..	1	1	..	..	..	..	..	..	..	1	1
,, 15 20 ,, ...	1	4	5	1	3	4	..	..	..	..	..	..
,, 20 30 ,, ...	6	10	16	1	6	7	5	..	5	1	1	2
,, 30 40 ,, ...	13	7	20	1	5	6	7	..	7	4	1	5
,, 40 50 ,, ...	14	7	21	3	2	5	13	1	14	3	4	7
,, 50 60 ,, ...	11	5	16	2	..	2	4	1	5	1	4	5
,, 60 70 ,, ...	2	6	8	1	1	2	3	1	4	4	5	9
,, 70 80 ,, ...	3	1	4	..	..	..	3	..	3	1	1	2
,, 80 90 ,, ...	..	1	1	..	..	..	1	..	1	..	1	1
,, 90 and upwards	..	..	..	..	..	..	..	..	..	..	..	..
,, Not ascertained	1	..	1	..	..	..	1	..	1	..	..	..
TOTAL...............	51	42	93	9	17	26	37	3	40	14	18	32

TABLE IX.

Condition as to Marriage in the Admissions, Discharges, and Deaths during the Year 1880.

Condition in Reference to Marriage.	The Admissions.			The Discharges.						The Deaths.		
				Recovered.			Removed (Relieved, or otherwise).					
	Male.	Female.	Total.	Male.	Female.	Total.	Male.	Female.	Total.	Male.	Female.	Total.
Single	32	19	51	2	8	10	26	..	26	5	7	12
Married	15	16	31	6	8	14	8	2	10	6	9	15
Widowed	3	7	10	1	1	2	2	1	3	3	2	5
Not ascertained	1	..	1	..	..	..	1	..	1	..	..	..
TOTAL	51	42	93	9	17	26	37	3	40	14	18	32

TABLE X.

Showing the Admissions and Deaths during each Month in the Year.

	Admissions.			Deaths.		
	Male.	Female.	Total.	Male.	Female.	Total.
January..	5	5	10	4	2	6
February	2	2	4	0	2	2
March	0	3	3	3	1	4
April	0	4	4	2	1	3
May	0	1	1	0	1	1
June	0	6	6	0	0	0
July	0	2	2	1	2	3
August	0	3	3	1	1	2
September	1	5	6	0	2	2
October	2	7	9	0	3	3
November	35	1	36	2	2	4
December	6	3	9	1	1	2
	51	42	93	14	18	32

TABLE XI.

Showing the form of Mental Disorder in those Admitted.

	Male.	Female.	Total.
Mania	15	13	28
,, Acute	3	8	11
,, Chronic	9	3	12
,, Epileptic	1	..	1
Melancholia..	2	5	7
Dementia..	12	6	18
,, Acute	..	..	..
,, Senile	..	3	3
,, Epileptic	1	1	2
General Paralysis	5	1	6
Imbecility	3	1	4
Idiocy	..	1	1
Total..	51	42	93

TABLE XII.

Summary of Meteorological Observations for 1880, *taken at Fulbourn Asylum,* 67 *feet above the Sea Level. Means of Observations for each Month.*

1880	Barometer corrected and reduced.	Temperature.		Humidity.	Rainfall.
		Max.	Min.		
January	30·353	40·2	27·2	30·6	·009
February	29·815	50·6	34·7	40·2	·057
March	30·105	56·4	32·3	40·2	·020
April	29·672	58·5	38·4	45·1	·073
May	30·070	68·1	39·4	49·1	·017
June	29·875	69·4	47·2	55·3	·082
July..	29·214	75·2	51·8	60·06	·145
August	29·975	73·8	53·8	59·9	·039
September	30·120	73·0	49·5	52·1	·080
October	29·625	55·7	37·9	44·3	·151
November	30·925	50·8	33·6	38·9	·065
December	29·878	48·2	35·2	39·4	·074

TABLE XIII.

Direction of Wind. *Rainfall.*

1879.	Number of Days.								Rainfall.		
	N	NW	NE	S	SW	SE	E	W	Total Depth.	Greatest Fall in 24 Hours.	Number of days on which ·01 inch or more fell.
									Inches.	Depth.	
January ..	1	4	1	8	3	5	3	6	·28	·06	6
February ..	1	1	1	10	6	3	..	7	1·67	·38	14
March	2	1	7	1	6	4	6	4	·64	·36	3
April	3	1	9	7	7	..	..	3	2·20	·42	15
May	6	5	10	1	5	1	2	1	·53	·27	5
June	4	4	5	2	6	..	3	6	2·49	·44	19
July	1	3	..	3	15	4	1	4	4·51	·60	22
August	13	7	4	1	3	..	2	1	1·22	·35	7
September..	1	9	2	3	6	4	..	5	2·60	1·24	9
October	5	4	3	2	2	2	3	10	3·74	1·42	16
November ..	2	6	1	2	13	1	1	4	1·96	·56	13
December ..	..	7	1	6	16	..	1	..	2·32	·29	17
Total.	39	52	44	46	88	24	22	51	24·16	6·39	146

ALSO FROM

CURIOUS PUBLICATIONS

The Embalmed Head of Oliver Cromwell: A Memoir
by Marc Hartzman

The History of Spiritualism (Vols. 1 & 2)
by Sir Arthur Conan Doyle

Psycho-Phone Messages
by Francis Grierson

Spectropia, or Surprising Spectral Illusions Showing Ghosts Everywhere
by J. H. Brown

Spirit Slate Writing and Kindred Phenomena
by William E. Robinson

The Sight of Hell
by Rev. John Furniss

How to Speak With the Dead: A Practical Handbook
by Sciens

The Talking Dead: A Collection of Messages from Beyond the Veil, 1850s-1920s
Edited by Marc Hartzman

Reminiscences of the Elephant Man
by Sir Frederick Treves and Others

Vampires and Vampirism
by Dudley Wright

The Life and Adventures of Toby the Sapient Pig
by Himself

CPSIA information can be obtained
at www.ICGtesting.com
Printed in the USA
BVHW031641220721
612633BV00008B/478

9 781735 320168